Friendship Bracelets

REBORN

From colorful and charmed to earthy and beaded, the 23 bracelets in this fun book make stylish jewelry that you and your friends will love wearing every day.

13

3

17

19

4

16

6

30

9

LEISURE ARTS, INC. • Maumelle, Arkansas

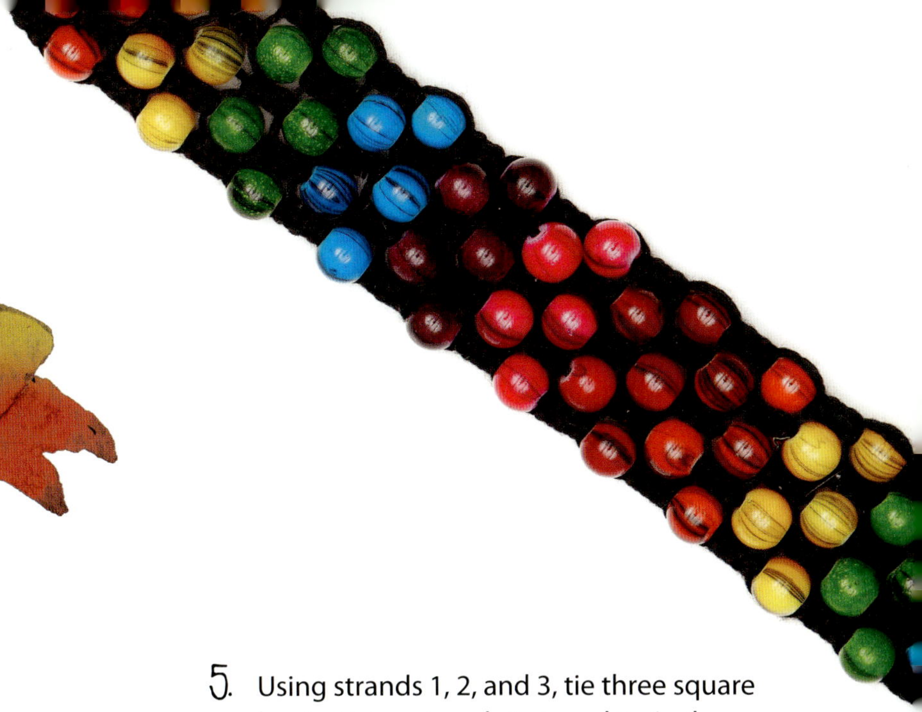

Beaded Cuff

You'll need:

- ☐ 2 skeins black embroidery floss
- ☐ 6mm beads (we used 65 assorted color beads for our 8" bracelet)

To make the bracelet:

1. Cut six 72" strands and five 15" strands of floss. Holding the ends together, tie an overhand knot (page 31) about 1/2" from one end. Divide the strands into 3 groups and braid them for about 2 1/2". Tie an overhand knot.

2. Tape the braid down and arrange the strands as shown in **Fig. 1**.

3. The square knots are tied using a group of three strands. In a group, the short strand is the center strand that the knots are tied around. Using strands 1, 2, and 3, tie three square knots (page 31). Using strands 5, 6, and 7, tie three square knots. Using strands 9, 10, and 11, tie three square knots.

4. Using strands 3, 4, and 5, tie three square knots. Using strands 7, 8, and 9, tie three square knots. Slide a bead on strands 2, 6, and 10 ***(Fig. 2)***.

Fig. 1

L = long
S = short

Fig. 2

5. Using strands 1, 2, and 3, tie three square knots. Using strands 5, 6, and 7, tie three square knots. Using strands 9, 10, and 11, tie three square knots. Slide a bead on strands 4 and 8 ***(Fig. 3)***.

Fig. 3

6. Repeat Steps 4-5 until the bracelet is the desired length, changing bead colors and ending with square knot groupings.

7. Holding all strands together, tie an overhand knot close to the last square knots made. Divide the strands into 2 groups. Divide each group into 3 parts. Braid each group for about 1". Holding all strands together, tie an overhand knot. Trim the floss ends.

Multi-Color Knotted Spiral

You'll need:

- ☐ green, blue, pink, purple & magenta embroidery floss

To make the bracelet:

1. Cut a 54" length of each floss color. Holding all floss strands together, fold them in half and tie an overhand knot (page 31) about 3/4" from the fold. Tape the loop down.

2. Use 2 matching floss strands together like a single strand. Knot the 2 green strands around all the other strands ***(Fig. 1)*** and tighten. Continue knotting ***(Fig. 2)*** for about 3/4". The knots will create a spiral.

Fig. 1

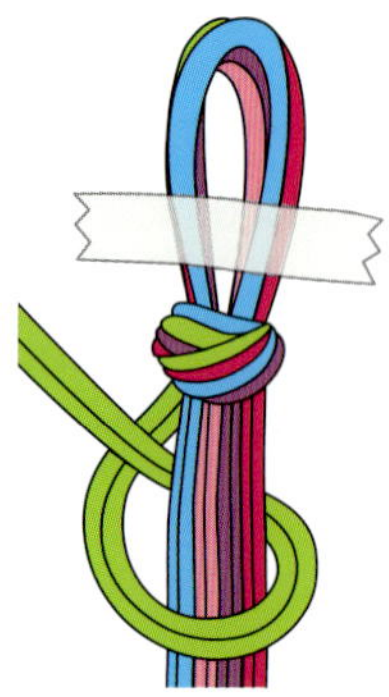

Fig. 2

3. Change to the 2 blue strands and continue knotting for about 3/4". Change to the pink strands for 3/4", then the purple strands for 3/4", and then the magenta strands for 3/4". Repeat this color order until the bracelet is the desired length.

4. Tie an overhand knot. Divide the strands into 2 groups and twist them in opposite directions. Now twist the two twisted groups together and tie an overhand knot. Trim the strands about 1 1/4" from the knot.

Two-Color Square Knot Spiral

You'll need:

- ☐ magenta & lavender embroidery floss
- ☐ 15 large-hole flat disc beads (a mix of bronze, gold & copper)

To make the bracelet:

1. Cut two 72" strands of each floss color. Holding all floss strands together, fold the strands in half and tie an overhand knot (page 31) about 3/4" from the fold. Tape the loop down.

2. Arrange the floss strands as shown in **Fig. 1**.

3. Use the outer lavender strands to make the first half of a square knot around the other strands ***(Fig. 2)***. Continue making half square knots for about 1 1/2". The knots will create a spiral.

Fig. 1

Fig. 2

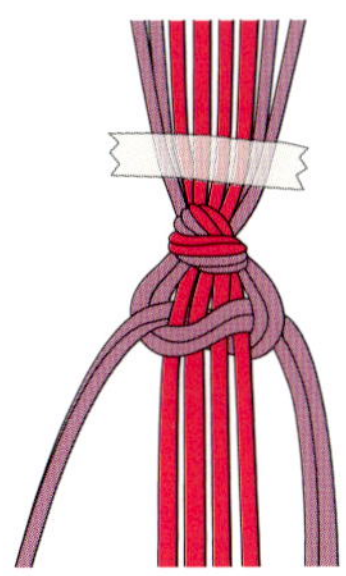

4. Slide 5 beads onto the bracelet. Switch the strands so that the magenta is on the outside and the lavender is in the center. Use the magenta strands to tie half square knots for about 1".

5. Repeat Step 4. Slide 5 beads onto the bracelet. Switch the strands so that the lavender is on the outside. Use the lavender strands to tie half square knots for about 1 1/2" or until the bracelet is the desired length. Tie an overhand knot close to the last square knot. Trim the ends about 4" from the knot.

Zig-Zag

You'll need:

- ☐ ecru, brown, light brown, aqua & green embroidery floss
- ☐ crystal charm with attached jump ring
- ☐ 2 pair of chain-nose pliers

To make the bracelet:

1. Cut a 36" strand of each color floss. Holding all floss strands together, tie an overhand knot (page 31) about 2" from one end. Tape the ends down.
2. Arrange the floss as shown in **Fig. 1**.
3. Starting on the left side with ecru, make left knots (page 31) across the remaining 4 strands ***(Fig. 2)***. *Remember to tie each knot twice!*
4. Starting again on the left side with brown, make left knots across the remaining 4 strands. *Remember to tie each knot twice!*
5. Always starting on the left, repeat Step 3 with aqua, green, and light brown. A diagonal pattern will form ***(Fig. 3)***.
6. Remove the tape; turn the bracelet over and tape down again.
7. Start again on the left side with light brown and knot across. Knot in pattern for a total of 6 rows ending with light brown ***(Fig. 4)***.
8. Repeat Steps 6-7 until bracelet is the desired length. Holding all strands together, tie an overhand knot and trim the strands about 2" from the knot.
9. Use the jump ring (page 32) to attach the charm to the bracelet.

Fig. 1

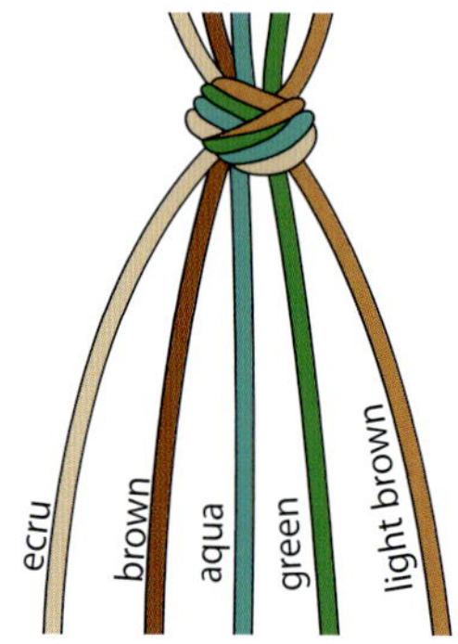

Fig. 2

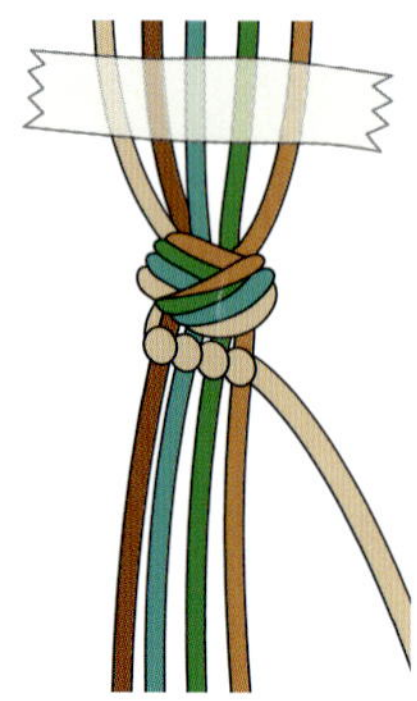

Fig. 3

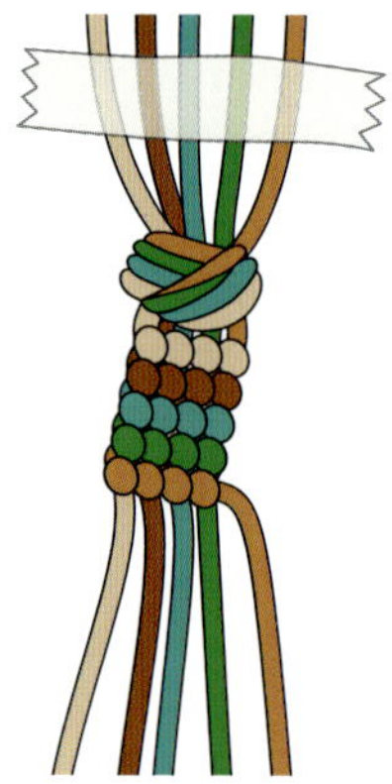

Fig. 4

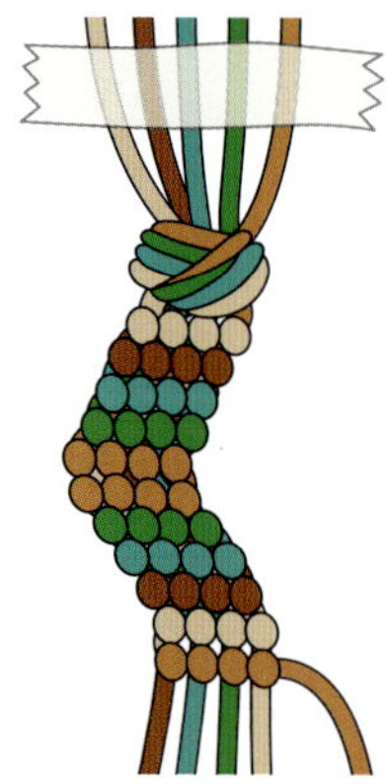

Charmed Diagonal

You'll need:

- ☐ orange, teal & dark yellow embroidery floss
- ☐ 3 charms with attached jump rings
- ☐ 2 pairs needle-nose pliers

To make the bracelet:

1. Cut a 72" length of each floss color. Holding all strands together, fold the strands in half and tie an overhand knot (page 31) about 3/4" from one end. Tape the loop down.

2. Arrange the floss strands as shown in **Fig. 1**. Starting on the left side with orange as the knotting strand, make left knots (page 31) across 5 strands ***(Fig. 2)***. *Remember to tie each knot twice!*

Fig. 1

Fig. 2

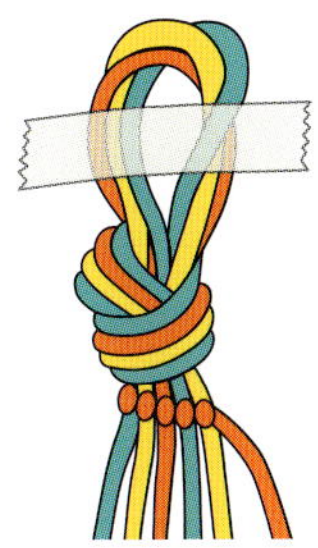

3. Start again on the left side and make left knots across 5 strands with teal. Always starting with the new left strand and working left to right, continue knotting until the bracelet is the right length. A diagonal pattern will form. Tie an overhand knot and trim the floss ends about 3" from the knot.

4. Open the jump ring (page 32) on a charm. Slide the open jump ring between the floss strands at the bracelet center. Close the jump ring. Repeat to add the remaining charms on either side of the center charm.

Diamond X's

You'll need:

- ☐ white & black embroidery floss
- ☐ 5/8" diameter shank-style button

To make the bracelet:

1. Cut a 90" strand of white floss and four 72" strands of black floss. Holding all floss strands together, fold the strands in half and tie an overhand knot (page 31) about 3/4" from the fold. Tape the loop down. Arrange the strands as shown in **Fig. 1**.

Fig. 1

2. Starting on the left side and referring to the key, make left and right knots (as shown on the chart) across Row 1. *Remember to tie each knot twice!*

3. Starting on the left side again and pulling the first left strand off to the left, make left and right knots across Row 2, pulling the last right strand off to the right.

4. Continue making knots across the rows until you complete Row 10. On Row 11, the first knot is a right, left knot: tie the first part of a right knot, then tie the second part of a left knot. The last knot on Row 11 is a left, right knot: tie the first part of a left knot, then tie the second part of a right knot. Make left and right knots across Row 12. You should have a white X on a black background.

5. Repeat Rows 1-12 until the bracelet is the desired length.

6. For the closure, thread half the floss strands through the button shank and tie on the back with the remaining floss strands. Trim the strands about 1 1/2" from the button.

Knotting Chart

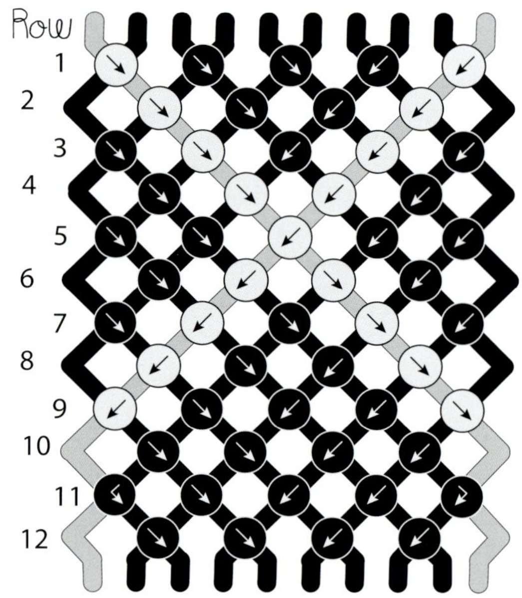

Knotting Key

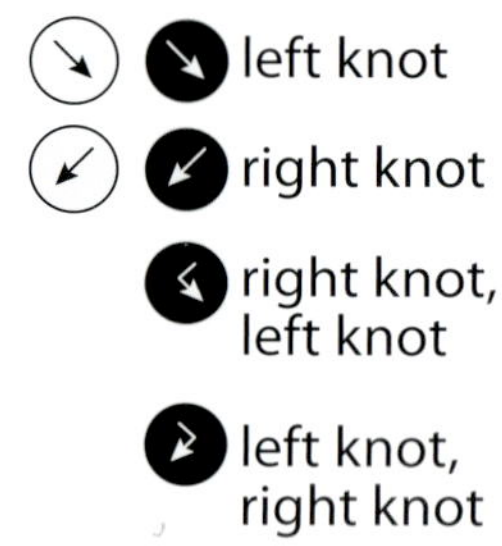

This bracelet uses a knotting chart to show the pattern. Refer to the key near the chart. It indicates the floss colors and types of knots. Start on the left side of each row and work all the way across that row. On rows where the first or last floss strand is pointing outward and not in a knot, you can just push those strands off to the side for that row. Instructions for left and right knots are on page 31.

Zig-Zag Crystals

You'll need:

- ☐ dark pink embroidery floss (2 skeins)
- ☐ 24 medium crystal faceted beads
- ☐ silver toggle clasp
- ☐ 8mm silver jump ring
- ☐ 5mm silver jump ring
- ☐ 2 sewing needles that will fit through the beads
- ☐ craft glue
- ☐ $2^{3}/_{4}$" x 2" cardboard piece

To make the bracelet:

1. Cut three 36" floss lengths and two 12" lengths. Using the bar piece of the toggle clasp and one 12" floss length, hold the three 36" lengths together and finish one end (page 32). The middle strand is the core strand that the knots are tied around.

2. Tape down the toggle bar. Tie a square knot (page 31) around the core strand. Tie another square knot ***(Fig. 1)***.

3. Thread a needle on each outer strand.

4. Slide a bead on the right strand. Tie a square knot under the bead ***(Fig. 2)***.

5. Slide a bead on the left strand. Tie a square knot under the bead ***(Fig. 3)***.

Fig. 1

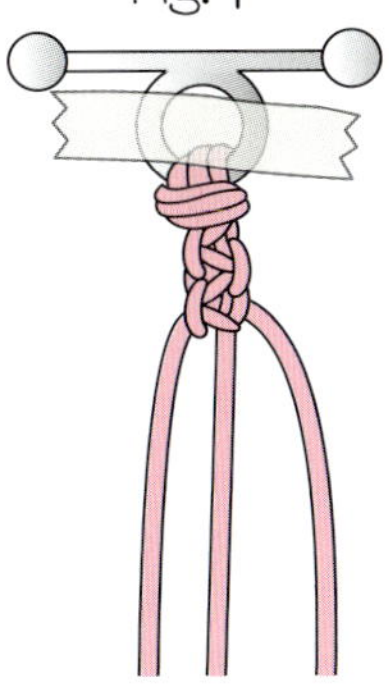

Fig. 2

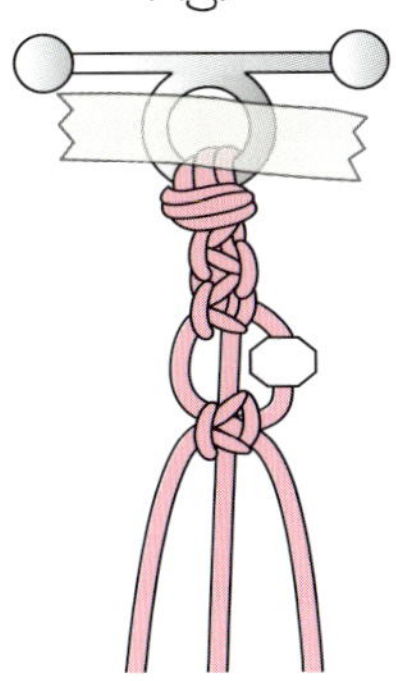

Fig. 3

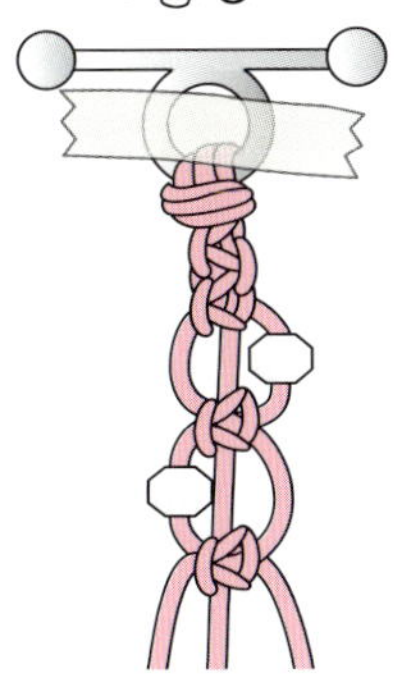

6. Alternating sides, continue adding beads and tying square knots until the bracelet is 1" shorter than the desired finished length.

7. Tie 2 square knots.

8. Finish the end with the remaining toggle clasp piece. Make a tassel (page 32) and use the 5mm jump ring to attach it to the clasp.

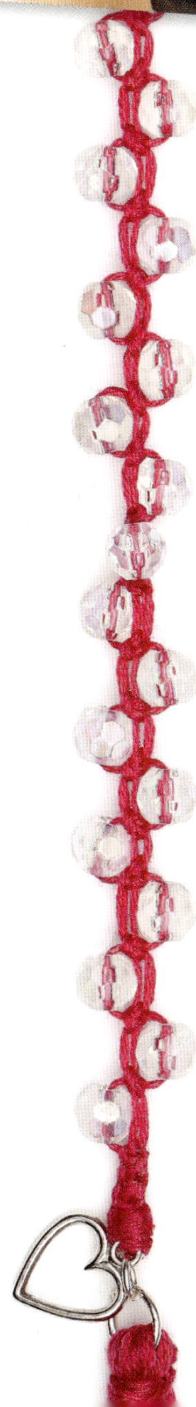

Tri-Color Square Knot

You'll need:

- ☐ very dark grey, grey & light grey embroidery floss
- ☐ 7/8" diameter silver metal ring
- ☐ 2 5/8" silver ribbon pinch clasps
- ☐ silver lobster clasp
- ☐ 2 pair of chain-nose pliers
- ☐ craft glue

To make the bracelet:

1. Hook the two clasp pieces together, measure the length, and add 1 1/4" for the ring and ribbon pinch clasps. Subtract the clasp/ring measurement from the desired finished bracelet size. Divide this measurement by two.

2. Cut two 36" very dark grey floss strands.

3. Fold the strands in half; attach to one side of the ring with a lark's head knot (page 31).

4. Tape the ring down. Tie square knots (page 31) around the 2 center strands ***(Fig. 1)*** until the knotted area is the measurement determined in Step 1. Tie a tight overhand knot very close to the last square knot. Apply a drop of glue to the knot. When the glue is dry, trim the floss ends close to the knot.

Fig. 1

5. Repeat Steps 2-4 with the grey and then the light grey floss.

6. Lay the knotted floss ends in the ribbon clasp and apply a bit of glue. Use the pliers to close the clasp over the knots.

7. Repeat Steps 2-6 for the other side of the bracelet.

8. Use jump rings (page 32) to attach the lobster clasp pieces to the ribbon clasps.

Alternating Color Square Knots

You'll need:

- ☐ blue, dark blue & white embroidery floss
- ☐ monogram & rhinestone charms with attached jump ring
- ☐ 2 pair chain-nose pliers

To make the bracelet:

1. Cut two 72" strands of each floss color.
2. Holding all the strands together, fold them in half and tie an overhand knot (page 31) about $\frac{3}{4}$" from the fold. Tape the loop down. Arrange the strands as shown in **Fig. 1**.
3. Use the dark blue strands to tie 8 square knots (page 31) around all the other strands.
4. Switch the strands so that the blue is on the outside and the dark blue is in the center with the white ***(Fig. 2)***. Use the blue strands to tie 8 square knots.

Fig. 1

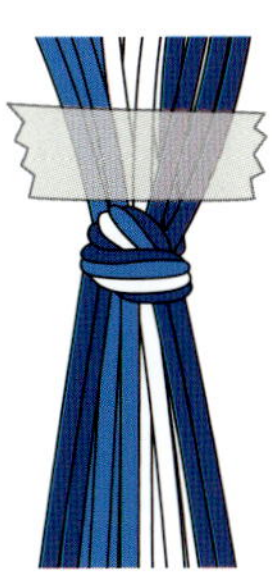

Fig. 2

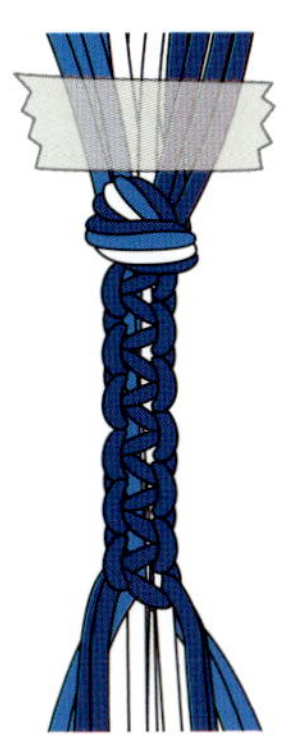

5. Switch the strands so that the white is on the outside and the blue is in the center with the dark blue. Use the white strands to tie 8 square knots.
6. Switch the strands so that the dark blue is on the outside and the white is in the center with the blue. Use the dark blue strands to tie 8 square knots.
7. Repeat Steps 4-6 until the bracelet is the desired length.
8. Tie an overhand knot close to the last square knot. Braid the ends for about 3". Tie an overhand knot. Trim the floss ends about $1\frac{1}{2}$" from the overhand knot.
9. Use the jump ring (page 32) to attach the charms to the bracelet.

Multi-Color Chevron

You'll need:

- ☐ blue, white & lime green embroidery floss

To make the bracelet:

1. Cut four 36" strands of blue floss and two 36" strands of white and lime green floss. Holding all floss strands together, tie an overhand knot (page 31) about $2\frac{1}{2}$" from one end. Tape the knot down.

2. Arrange the floss strands as shown in **Fig. 1**. Starting on the left side and working toward the middle, make left knots (page 31) with blue across 3 strands ***(Fig. 2)***. *Remember to tie each knot twice!*

3. Starting on the right side and working toward the middle, make right knots (page 31) with blue across 3 strands ***(Fig. 3)***. *Remember to tie each knot twice!*

4. Now make a right knot in the middle forming the chevron "V" ***(Fig. 4)***.

Fig. 1

Fig. 2

Fig. 3

Fig. 4

5. Start again on the left side and make left knots with the next blue across 3 strands. Make right knots with the next blue across 3 strands and the blue right knot in the middle. Continue knotting until the bracelet is the desired length, always working toward the middle with the new outside strands. The chevron pattern will form.

6. Holding all strands together, tie an overhand knot and trim the strands about $2\frac{1}{2}$" from the knot.

Peacock Feather

You'll need:

- ☐ teal, blue, purple & black embroidery floss

To make the bracelet:

1. Cut two 54" lengths of each color floss. Holding all floss strands together, tie an overhand knot (page 31) about $2\frac{1}{2}$" from one end. Tape the knot down.

2. Arrange the floss as shown in **Fig. 1**.

3. Starting on the left side and working toward the middle, make left knots (page 31) with black across 3 strands ***(Fig. 2)***. *Remember to tie each knot twice!*

4. Starting on the right side and working toward the middle, make right knots (page 31) with black across 3 strands ***(Fig. 3)***. *Remember to tie each knot twice!*

5. Make a right knot with black on black in the center forming the chevron "V" ***(Fig. 4)***.

6. Start again on the left side and make left knots with teal across 3 strands. Make right knots with teal across 3 strands and a teal right knot in the center ***(Fig. 5)***.

7. Repeat Step 6 with blue and then with purple.

8. On the left side, make a left knot and then a right knot with black onto teal. On the right side, make a right knot and then a left knot with black onto teal ***(Fig. 6)***.

9. Starting in the center with the left purple strand and working toward the left, make right knots across the next 3 strands. Starting with the right purple strand and working toward the right, make left knots across the next 3 strands, forming a purple "X" ***(Fig. 7)***.

Fig. 1

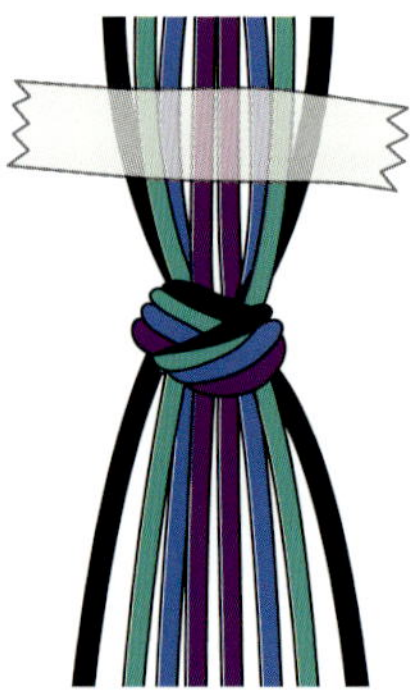

Fig. 2

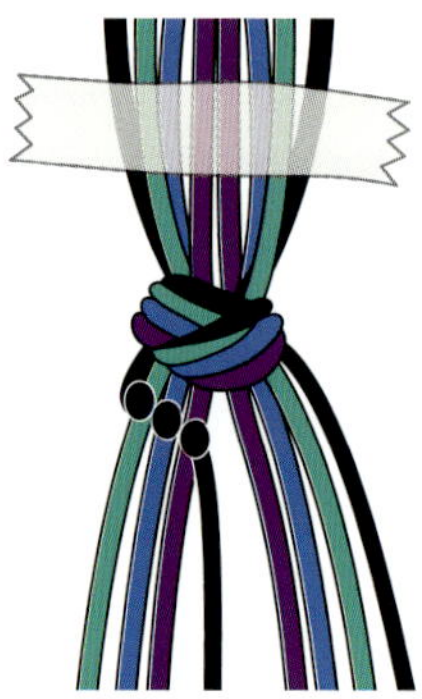

Fig. 3

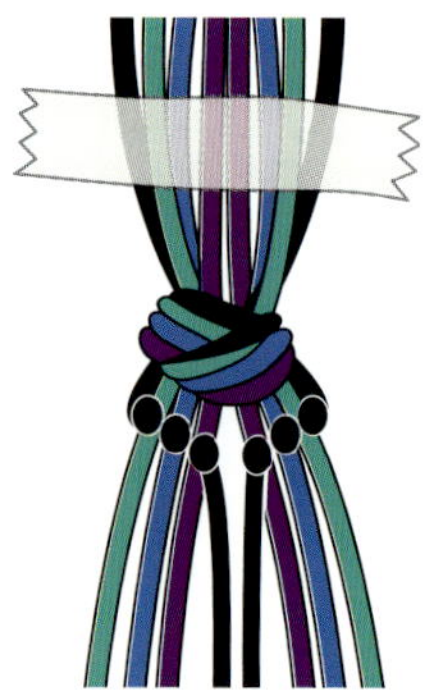

Fig. 4

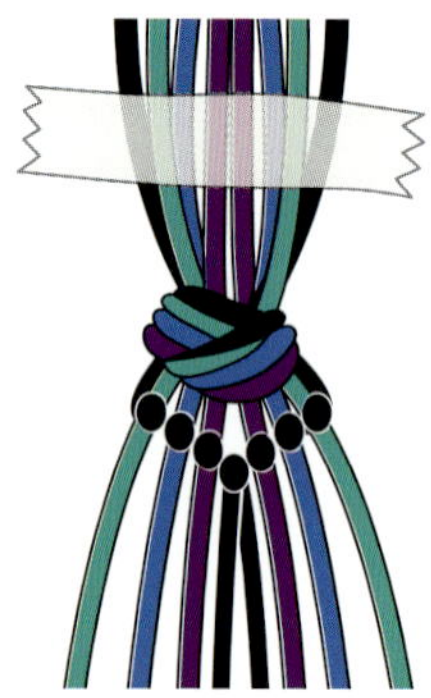

Fig. 5

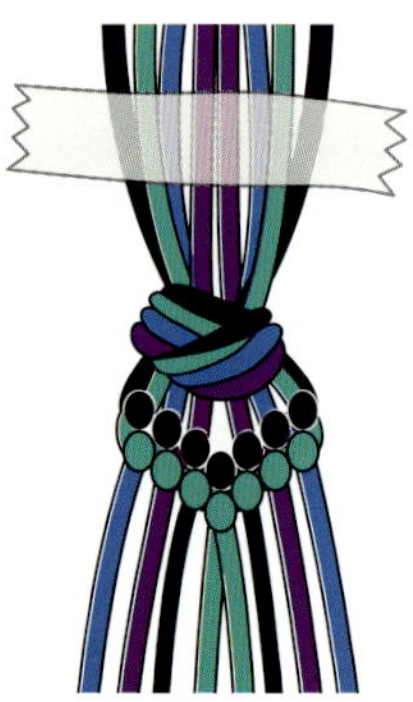

Fig. 6

Fig. 7

10. Make a right knot with blue on blue in the center. With the left blue strand, make right knots across the next 2 strands. With the right blue strand, make left knots across the next 2 strands. Repeat with teal to make center knot and to make left and right knots onto the black strands. Make a right knot with black on black in the center ***(Fig. 8)***.

11. Make a left knot with the left teal strand onto the left black strand. Make a right knot with the right teal strand onto the right black strand. Make a center knot with teal on teal ***(Fig. 9)***.

12. Repeat Step 11 with blue across 2 strands and with purple across 3 strands ***(Fig. 10)***.

13. Repeat Steps 8-12 until the bracelet is 1" shorter than the desired length.

14. Work Steps 3-7 in reverse order to complete the bracelet. Tie an overhand knot and trim the strands about 2 1/2" from the knot.

Fig. 8

Fig. 9

Fig. 10

Tasseled Two-Color Square Knot

You'll need:

- ☐ blue & purple embroidery floss (2 skeins of each color)
- ☐ 5 8mm silver jump rings
- ☐ 5 5mm silver jump rings
- ☐ 2 pair chain-nose pliers
- ☐ 2 3/4" x 2" cardboard piece

To make the bracelet:

1. Cut one 72" strand of each floss color; cut an 18" strand of each floss color. Fold the long strands in half; match the ends of the shorter strands to the fold center. Tie an overhand knot (page 31) about 3/4" from the fold. Tape the loop down and arrange the strands as shown in **Fig. 1**. The four center strands are the core strands that the knots are tied around. Tape the core strands down at the opposite end.

2. Use the blue and purple strands to make square knots around the center strands ***(Figs. 2-3)***. Continue making square knots until the bracelet is the desired length.

Fig. 1

Fig. 2

Fig. 3

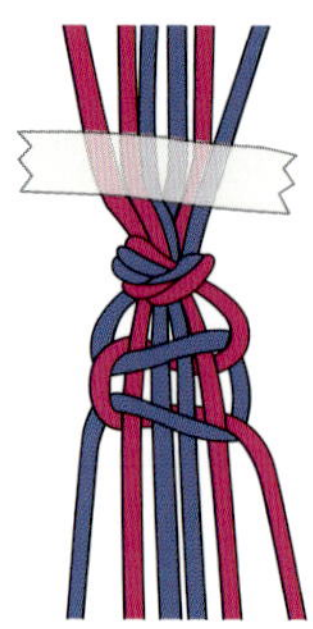

3. Holding all strands together, tie an overhand knot and trim the strands about 3" from the knot.

4. Make 3 blue and 2 purple tassels (page 32). Use a 5mm jump ring (page 32) to attach each tassel to the bracelet.

Wide Multi-Color Chevron

You'll need:

- ☐ magenta, yellow, light green, white & aqua embroidery floss
- ☐ 7/8" diameter shank-style flower button

To make the bracelet:

1. Cut four 36" strands of magenta and yellow floss and two 36" strands of light green, white, and aqua floss. Holding all floss strands together, tie an overhand knot (page 31) about 3" from one end. Tape the knot down.

2. Arrange the floss strands as shown in **Fig. 1**.

3. Starting on the left side and working toward the middle, make left knots (page 31) with magenta across 6 strands ***(Fig. 2)***. *Remember to tie each knot twice!*

4. Starting on the right side and working toward the middle, make right knots (page 31) with magenta across 6 strands ***(Fig. 3)***. *Remember to tie each knot twice!*

5. Now make a right knot in the center forming the chevron "V" ***(Fig. 4)***.

6. Start again on the left side and make left knots with the outer magenta strand across 6 strands. Make right knots with the outer magenta strand across 6 strands and the magenta right knot in the middle. Continue knotting until the bracelet is the desired length, always working toward the middle with the new outside strands. The chevron pattern will form.

7. Holding all strands together, tie an overhand knot. Divide the strands into 2 groups of 7 strands each. Divide these into 2 groups of 2 strands and 1 group of 3 strands. Braid each section for about 3"; tie an overhand knot and trim the floss about 1 1/2" from the knot.

8. For the closure, knot the braids together about 1" from the knot that secures the chevron part of the bracelet. On the opposite end, thread half the floss strands through the button shank and tie on the back with the remaining floss strands. Trim the strands close to the button.

Fig. 1

Fig. 2

Fig. 3

Fig. 4

Glass Bead

You'll need:

- ☐ cream embroidery floss
- ☐ 8mm beads (we used 9)

To make the bracelet:

1. Cut three 72" strands of floss.

2. Holding the ends together, fold the strands in half. Tie an overhand knot (page 31) about 3/4" from the fold; tape down the loop.

3. Use the 2 outer strands on each side to tie 4 square knots (page 31) around the 2 center strands.

4. Thread a bead on the center strands ***(Fig. 1)***. Tie 2 square knots.

Fig. 1

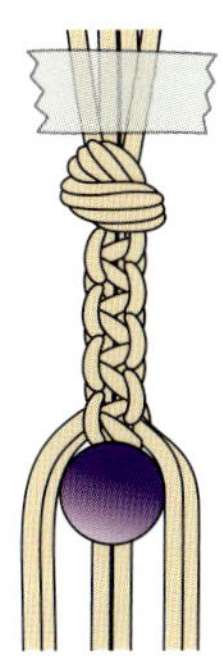

5. Repeat Step 4 to continue adding beads and tying square knots until the knotted area of the bracelet is about 6 1/2" long. Tie 2 more square knots.

6. Tie an overhand knot close to the last square knot. Trim the thread ends about 4" from the overhand knot.

Ladder

You'll need:

- ☐ brown embroidery floss
- ☐ 6mm x 7mm wood beads (we used 14 of one color & 12 of a second color)
- ☐ 2 sewing needles that will fit through the beads

To make the bracelet:

1. Cut four 72" long floss lengths. Holding the ends together, fold the lengths in half. Tie an overhand knot (page 31) about 3/4" from the fold; tape down the loop.

2. Use the 2 outer strands on each side to tie 3 square knots (page 31) around the four center strands.

3. Thread a needle on each set of 2 outer strands. Slide a bead on each outer strand set and tie 2 square knots.

4. Repeat Step 3 until bracelet is the desired length, alternating bead colors. Tie one more square knot.

5. Tie an overhand knot close to the last square knot and trim the strands about 4 1/2" from the knot.

Falling Leaves

You'll need:

- ☐ magenta, lime green, yellow, teal & aqua embroidery floss
- ☐ 1" diameter flower button

To make the bracelet:

1. Cut a 72" length of each floss color. Holding all floss lengths together, fold the strands in half and tie an overhand knot (page 31) about $1\frac{1}{4}$" from the fold. Tape the loop down.

2. Arrange the strands as shown in **Fig. 1**. Starting in the middle, make a right knot (page 31) with the aqua strands ***(Fig. 2)***. *Remember to tie the knot twice!*

3. Make a left knot (page 31) with the left teal strand on the left center aqua strand; make a right knot with the right teal strand on the right center aqua strand. Make a right knot with the teal strands ***(Fig. 3)***. *Remember to tie each knot twice!*

4. Make 2 left knots toward the middle with the left yellow strand; make 2 right knots toward the middle with the right yellow strand. Make a right knot with the yellow strands ***(Fig. 4)***.

5. Make 3 left knots toward the middle with the left lime green strand; make 3 right knots toward the middle with the right lime green strand. Make a right knot with the lime green strands ***(Fig. 5)***.

Fig. 1

Fig. 2

Fig. 3

Fig. 4

6. Make 4 left knots toward the middle with the left magenta strand; make 4 right knots toward the middle with the right magenta strand. Make a right knot with the magenta strands ***(Fig. 6)***.

7. Repeat Step 3 with the lime green strands.

8. Repeat Step 4 with the yellow strands.

9. Repeat Step 5 with the teal strands.

10. Repeat Step 6 with the aqua strands.

11. Repeat Steps 3-10 until the bracelet is the desired length. Tie an overhand knot.

12. For the closure, thread half the floss strands through the button holes and tie on the back with the remaining floss strands. Trim the strands.

Fig. 5

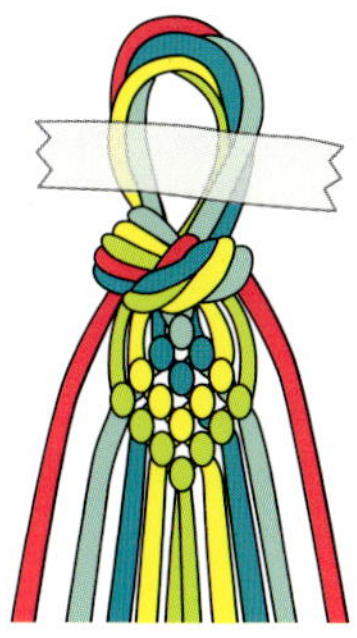

Fig. 6

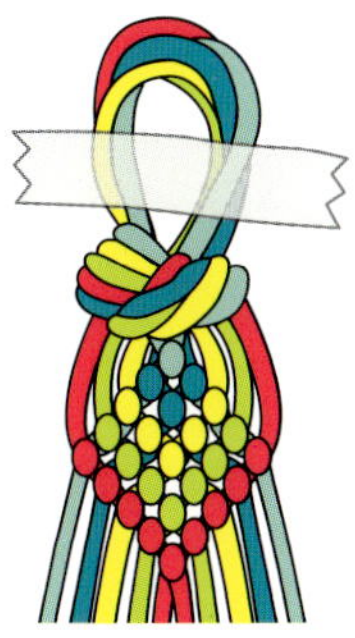

Skinny Chevron

You'll need:

- ☐ cream, yellow, orange, gold & brown embroidery floss
- ☐ charm with attached jump ring
- ☐ 2 pair of chain-nose pliers

To make the bracelet:

1. Cut two 36" lengths of each color floss. Holding all floss strands together, tie an overhand knot (page 31) about 2 1/2" from one end. Tape the knot down.

2. Arrange the floss as shown in **Fig. 1**.

3. Using two matching strands as a single strand and starting on the left side, make a left knot (page 31) with cream onto orange. *Remember to tie each knot twice!* Repeat with cream onto gold ***(Fig. 2)***.

4. Starting on the right side, make a right knot (page 31) with yellow onto brown. *Remember to tie each knot twice!* Repeat with yellow onto cream. A chevron pattern will form ***(Fig. 3)***.

5. Go back to the left side and make a left knot with orange on gold and then orange on yellow. On the right side make a right knot with brown on cream and then brown on orange ***(Fig. 4)***.

Fig. 1 Fig. 2 Fig. 3 Fig. 4

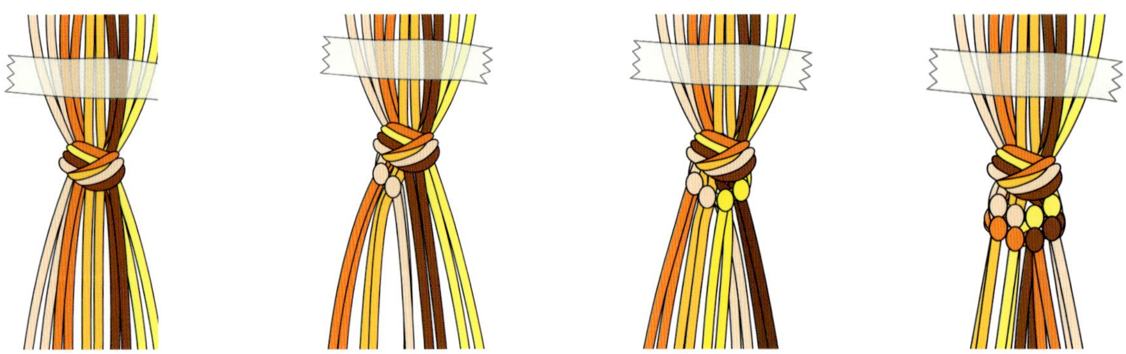

6. Alternating left and right sides, continue knotting in pattern until the bracelet is the desired length. Tie an overhand knot and trim the strands about 2 1/2" from the knot.

7. Use the jump ring (page 32) to attach the charm to the bracelet center.

Simple Tri-Color Braid

You'll need:

- ☐ red, white & blue embroidery floss

To make the bracelet:

1. Cut three 36" strands of each floss color. Holding all the strands together, fold them in half and tie an overhand knot (page 31) about 3/4" from the fold. Tape the loop down.

2. Separate the strands into 3 groups, keeping the same colors together. To braid, take the left strands over the middle strands; then take the right strands over the new middle strands ***(Fig. 1)***.

3. Keep braiding, alternating between the left and right strands ***(Fig. 2)*** and tightening the braid as you go, until the bracelet is the desired length. To end the bracelet, tie an overhand knot and trim the strands about 3 1/2" from the knot.

Fig. 1

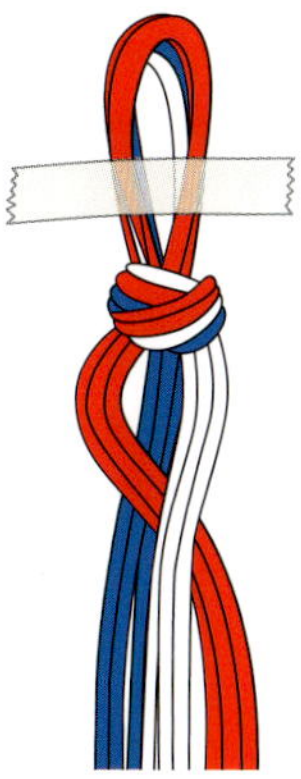

Fig. 2

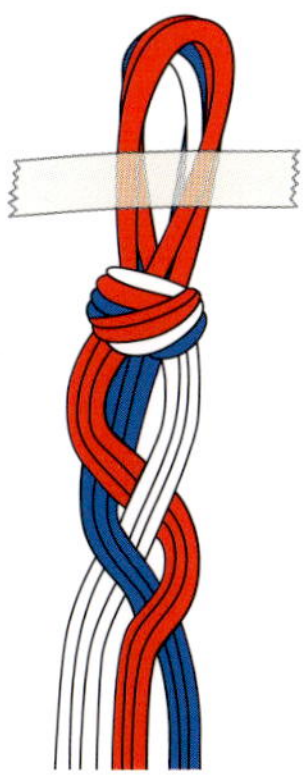

Half-Square Knot Spiral

You'll need:

- ☐ yellow embroidery floss
- ☐ 3 large-hole silver beads/charms

To make the bracelet:

1. Cut three 72" strands of floss. Holding all floss strands together, fold them in half and tie an overhand knot (page 31) about 3/4" from the fold; tie another knot over the first knot. Tape the knot down.

2. Use the outer strands to make the first half of a square knot around the center strands ***(Fig. 1)***. Continue making half square knots until the bracelet is the desired length. The knots will create a spiral.

Fig. 1

3. Slide the beads/charms onto the bracelet. Holding all strands together, tie an overhand knot; tie another knot over the first knot. Trim the strands about 4" from the knot.

Rainbow Diagonal

You'll need:

- ☐ red, yellow, orange, blue, purple & white embroidery floss

Knotting Chart

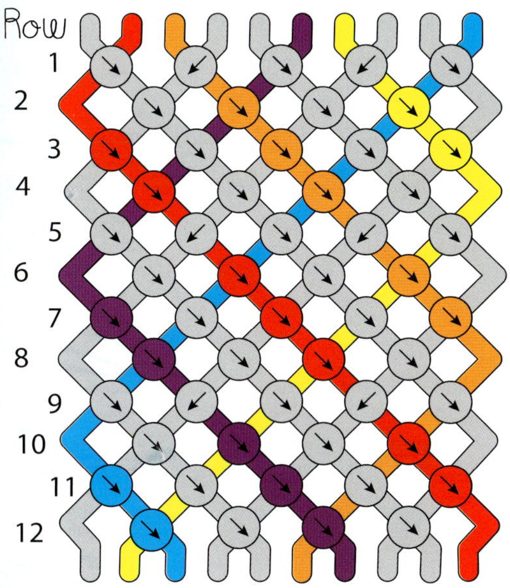

Knotting Key

↘ left knot

↙ right knot

For this bracelet there is a Chart with arrows indicating the direction to tie the knots. Pay close attention to the direction of the arrows. On even numbered rows the first and last strands are not used. They are picked up again on the next odd row.

To make the bracelet:

1. Cut five 36" lengths of white floss and one 36" length of each remaining floss color. Holding all floss strands together, tie an overhand knot (page 31) about 2" from one end. Tape the knot down.

2. Arrange the floss as shown in **Fig. 1**.

Fig. 1

3. Starting on the left side on Row 1, follow the Knotting Chart to make a left knot (page 31) with white onto red, a right knot (page 31) with white onto orange, a left knot with white onto purple, a right knot with white onto yellow, and a left knot with white onto blue. *Remember to tie each knot twice!*

4. Starting again on the left side on Row 2, follow the Knotting Chart to make a left knot with white onto white, orange onto purple, white onto white, and yellow onto blue. *Remember to tie each knot twice!*

5. Always starting on the left, follow the Knotting Chart for Rows 3-12. Continue knotting in pattern, repeating Rows 1-12, until the bracelet is the length you desire.

6. Tie an overhand knot and trim the strands about 2" from the knot.

Double Chevron

You'll need:

☐ white, yellow, green & blue embroidery floss

To make the bracelet:

1. Cut two 72" lengths of each color floss. Holding all the floss strands together, tie an overhand knot (page 31) about 2" from one end. Tape the knot down.
2. Arrange the floss and separate into 4 groups as shown in **Figs. 1-2**.
3. Starting on the left side of Group 1 with yellow, make left knots (page 31) across the remaining 3 strands ***(Fig. 3)***. *Remember to tie each knot twice!*
4. Starting on the right side of Group 2 with yellow, make right knots (page 31) across the remaining 3 strands ***(Fig. 4)***. *Remember to tie each knot twice!*
5. Make a right knot with the 2 yellow center strands ***(Fig. 5)***.
6. Starting on the left side of Group 1 with green, repeat Steps 3-5 ***(Fig. 6)***.

Fig. 1

Fig. 2

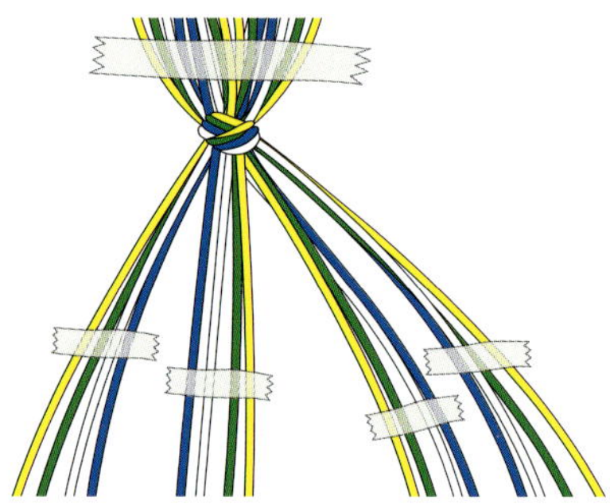

Fig. 3

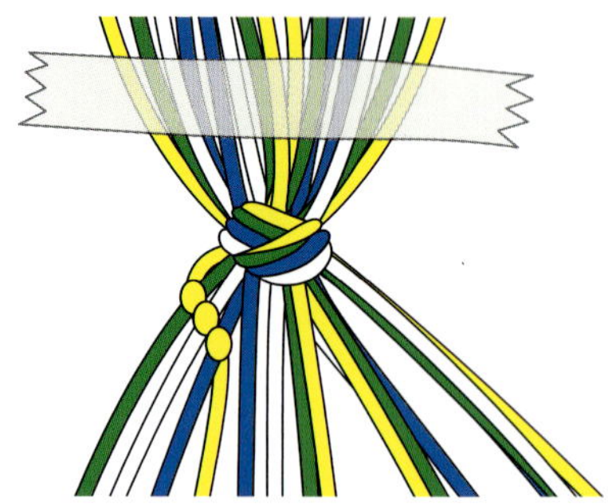

Fig. 4

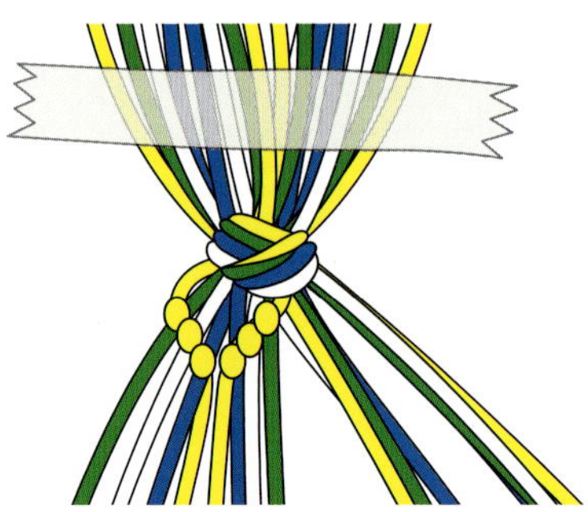

Fig. 5

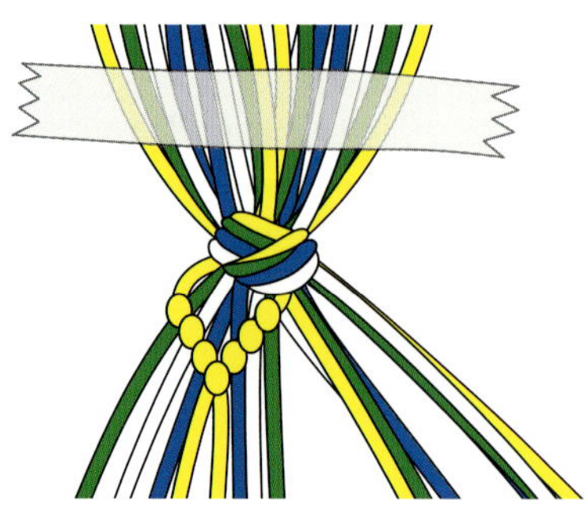

Fig. 6

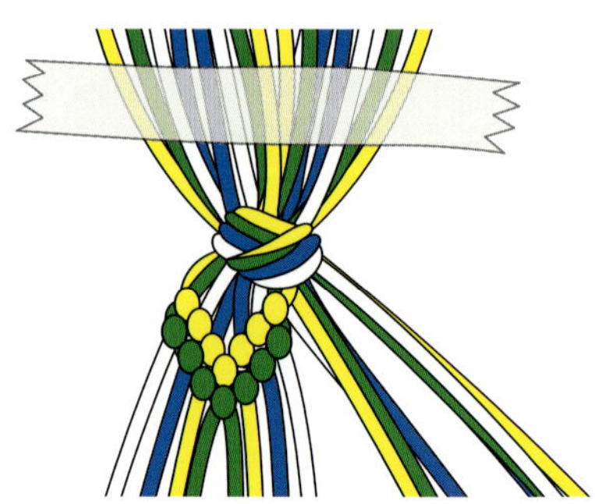

7. Repeat Steps 3-6 with Group 3 and Group 4 ***(Fig. 7)***.

8. At this point there is a left V and a right V. To connect the V's, tie a right knot with the 2 white center strands (1 from Group 2 and 1 from Group 3) as shown in **Fig. 8**.

9. Starting on the left side of Group 1 with white, make left knots across the remaining 3 strands. Starting on the right side of Group 2 with white, make right knots across the remaining 3 strands. Make a right knot with the 2 white center strands. Repeat for Groups 3-4 ***(Fig. 9)***.

10. Repeat Step 8 to join the 2 blue center strands and Step 9 to tie the blue row ***(Fig. 10)***.

11. Continue in pattern, repeating Steps 8-9 until bracelet is the desired length. Holding all strands together, tie an overhand knot.

12. Divide the strands into 2 groups; tie an overhand knot under each V. Braid each strand group for about $2^1/_2$". Tie an overhand knot and trim the strands about 1" from the knots.

Fig. 7

Fig. 8

Fig. 9

Fig. 10

Hearts

You'll need:

☐ red & light blue embroidery floss

To make the bracelet:

1. Cut two 72" strands of each floss color. Holding all floss strands together, fold the strands in half and tie an overhand knot (page 31) about 3/4" from the fold. Tape the loop down.

2. Arrange the floss strands as shown in **Fig. 1**. Starting on the left side and working toward the middle, make left knots (page 31) with red across 3 strands ***(Fig. 2)***. *Remember to tie each knot twice!*

3. Starting on the right side and working toward the middle, make right knots (page 31) with red across 3 strands ***(Fig. 3)***. *Remember to tie each knot twice!*

4. Now make a red right knot in the center forming the chevron "V" ***(Fig. 4)***.

Fig. 1

Fig. 2

Fig. 3

Fig. 4

5. Start again on the left side and make left knots with the light blue across 3 strands. Start again on the right side and make right knots with the light blue across 3 strands. Make a light blue right knot in the middle ***(Fig. 5)***.

6. Now take the light blue strand on the left side and make a right knot on the outer left red strand; make a left knot with the light blue strand on the right side on the outer right red strand ***(Fig. 6)***.

7. Start again on the left side and make left knots with the 1st red strand across 2 strands. Start again on the right side and make right knots with the 1st red strand across 2 strands. Make a red right knot in the middle ***(Fig. 7)***.

8. Take the red 2nd strand on the left and make a right knot on the light blue 1st strand. Take the red 7th strand and make a left knot on the light blue 8th strand. Make left knots with the light blue 2nd strand across 2 strands. Make right knots with the light blue 7th strand across 2 strands. Make a light blue right knot in the middle ***(Fig. 8)***.

9. Starting on the left side and working toward the middle, make left knots with red across 3 strands. Starting on the right side and working toward the middle, make right knots with red across 3 strands. Tie a right knot with the red strands in the middle ***(Fig. 9)***.

10. Continue knotting, repeating Steps 5-9, until the bracelet is the desired length. Holding all strands together, tie an overhand knot and trim the strands about $3^{1}/_{2}$" from the knot.

Fig. 5

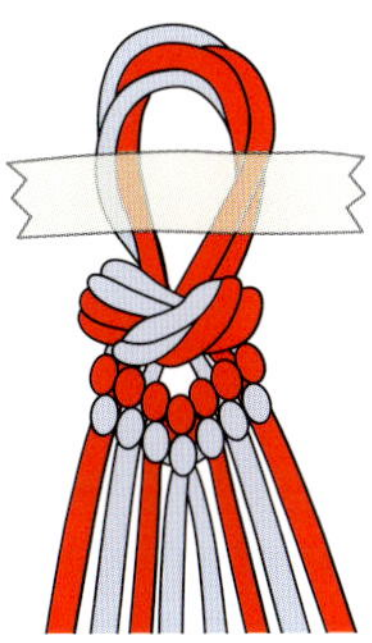

Fig. 6

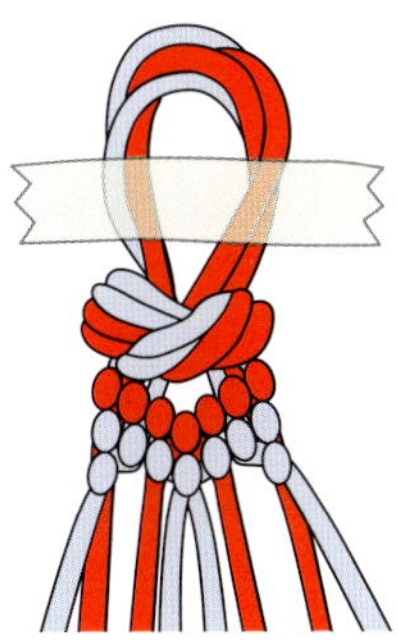

Fig. 7

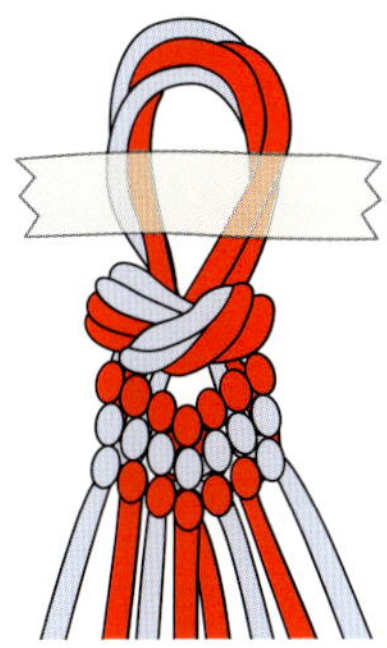

Fig. 8

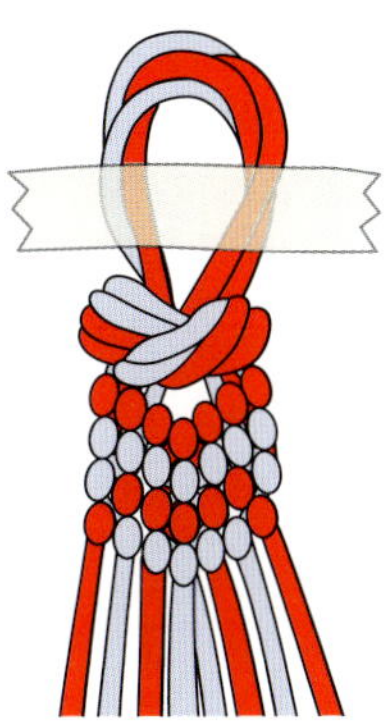

Fig. 9

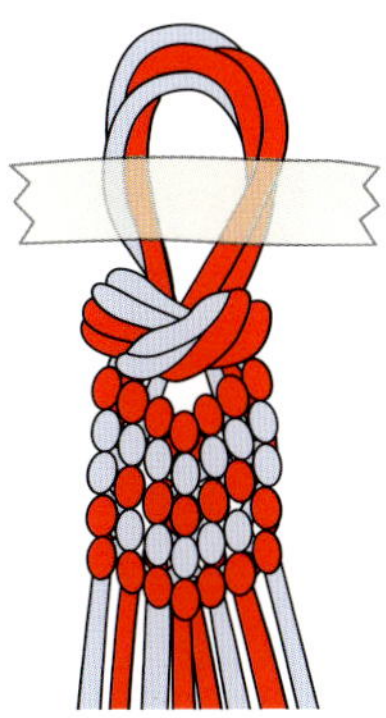

Blue Charms

You'll need:

- ☐ dark blue embroidery floss
- ☐ 7/8" diameter silver metal ring
- ☐ 7 silver beads
- ☐ 3 silver charms
- ☐ toggle clasp
- ☐ 3 8mm silver jump rings
- ☐ sewing needle that will fit through the beads
- ☐ 2 pair of chain-nose pliers
- ☐ craft glue

To make the bracelet:

1. Hook the two clasp pieces together, measure the length, and add 7/8" for the ring. Subtract the clasp/ring measurement from the desired finished bracelet size. Divide this measurement by two.

2. Cut four 48", one 24", and two 12" floss lengths.

3. The 24" strand is the core strand that the knots are tied around. Thread the needle on the core strand. Slide a bead to the center of the core strand. Place the core strand across the ring with the bead centered in the ring ***(Fig. 1)***. Be sure the needle is facing you.

4. Fold two 48" strands in half; attach to one side of the ring with a lark's head knot (page 31), over the core strand ***(Fig. 2)***. Repeat for the other side using the 2 remaining 48" strands.

Fig. 1

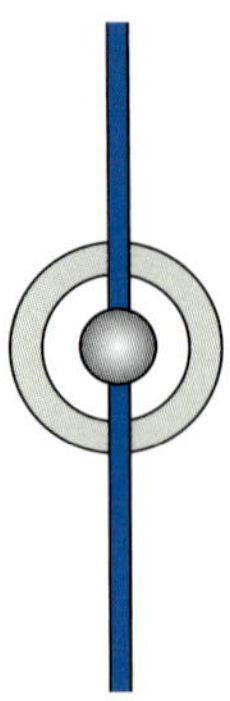

Fig. 2

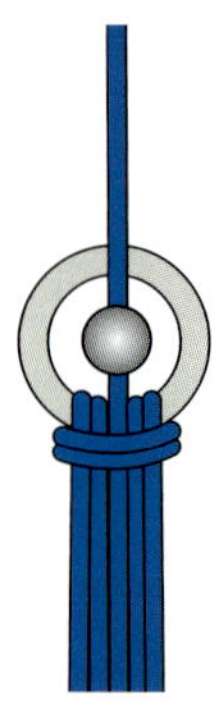

5. Tape down the strands. Holding 2 strands together as one, tie 3 square knots (page 31) around the core strand on one side of the bracelet ***(Fig. 3)***.

Fig. 3

6. Slide a bead on the core strand and tie 3 more square knots. Slide another bead on the core strand and tie 3 square knots; repeat. Continue to tie square knots until the bracelet is the measurement determined in Step 1.

7. Remove the needle. Trim the strand ends to 2" and finish the ends (page 32) using a toggle clasp piece and a 12" floss length.

8. Repeat Steps 5-7 for the other side of the bracelet, threading the needle on the core strand before beginning.

9. Use jump rings (page 32) to attach the charms to the ring.

General Instructions

KNOTS

Overhand Knot – loose or folded ends

Hold the strands together and tie a knot before taping the strands to the work surface ***(Figs. 1-2)***.

Fig. 1

Fig. 2

Lark's Head Knot

Slip the loop through the metal ring from the front. Pull the ends through the loop and tighten ***(Fig. 3)***.

Fig. 3

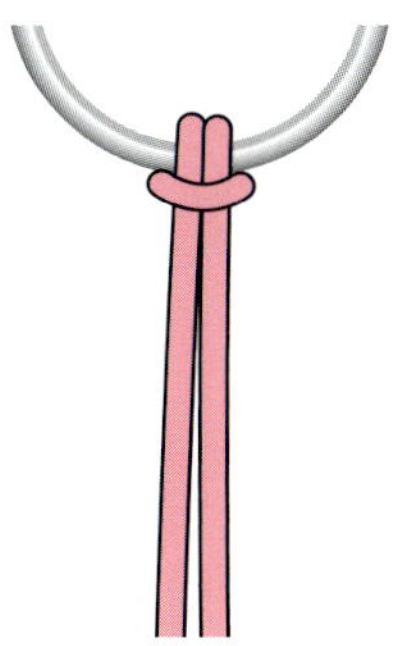

Square Knot

Use the outer strand(s) to tie the first half of a square knot ***(Fig. 4)***.

Use the outer strand(s) to tie the second half of a square knot ***(Fig. 5)***.

Fig. 4

Fig. 5

Half-Square Knot

Refer to **Fig. 4** to tie the first half only of a square knot; repeat until you reach the desired length. As you tie, the knots will spiral.

Left Knot

Begin with the strand(s) on the left side. Wrap these around the center strand(s) and pull upward to tighten. To complete each left knot, always tie again, using the same strand(s) ***(Figs. 6-7)***.

Fig. 6

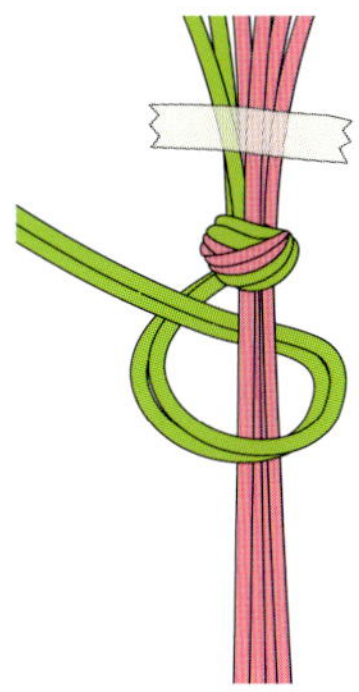

Fig. 7

Right Knot

Begin with the strand(s) on the right side. Wrap these around the center strand(s) and pull upward to tighten. To complete each right knot, always tie again, using the same strand(s) ***(Figs. 8-9)***.

Fig. 8

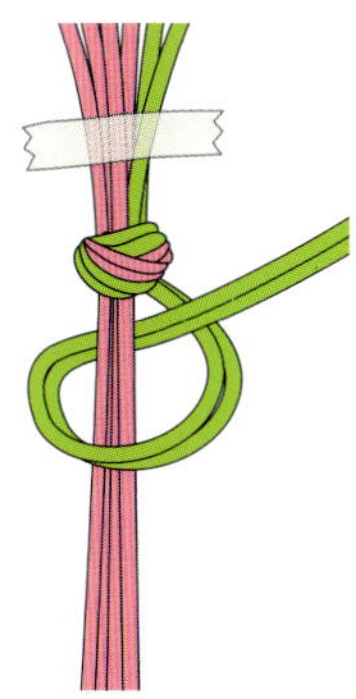

Fig. 9

Using Jump Rings

Pick up a jump ring with a pair of chain-nose pliers. With a second pair of chain-nose pliers, gently hold the other side of the ring. Open the ring by pulling one pair of pliers toward you while pushing the other away ***(Fig. 10)***.

Fig. 10

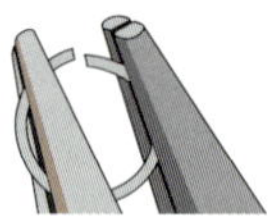

Close the ring by pushing and pulling the pliers in opposite directions, bringing the ring ends back together.

Finishing Ends

Holding the strands together and leaving 1" tails, fold the floss over a jump ring or clasp ***(Fig. 11)***.

Fig. 11

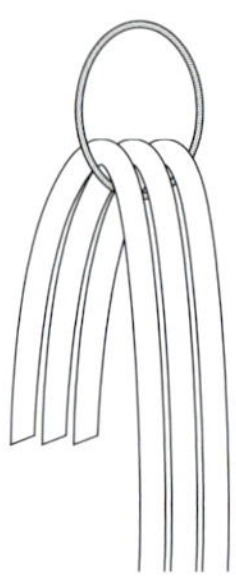

Form a loop with a 12" length of floss. Wrap the length around the folded strands 4-5 times. Bring the end through the loop. Pull firmly on the opposite end of the cord until the loop disappears ***(Fig. 12)***.

Fig. 12

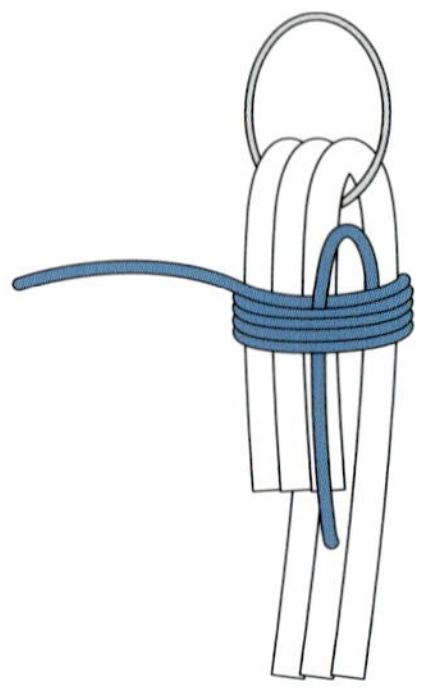

Place a drop of glue on the knot. When the glue is dry, trim the ends ***(Fig. 13)***.

Fig. 13

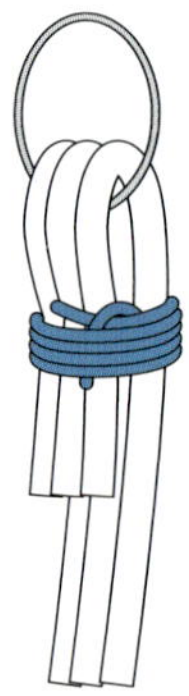

Making a Tassel

Wrap floss around the cardboard about 25 times. Trim the floss from the skein. Open an 8mm jump ring and slip it behind the wraps. Bring the ring to the top of the cardboard and close the ring. Cut the floss loops on the end opposite the jump ring ***(Fig. 14)***.

Fig. 14

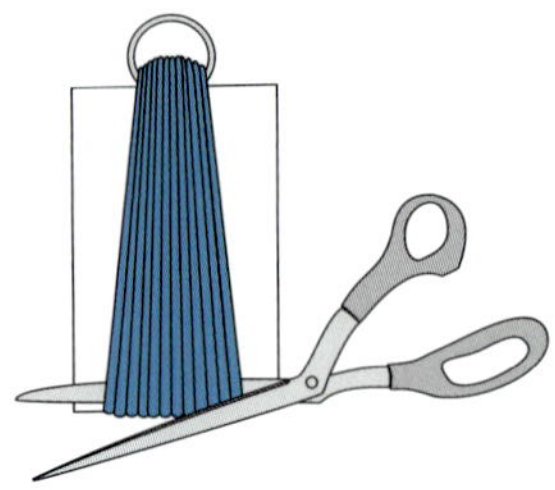

Remove the cardboard. Holding the floss ends together, tie a 10" floss length around the tassel about 1/4" below the jump ring ***(Fig. 15)***. Trim all floss ends.

Fig. 15

Production Team: Designer – Kelly Reider; Technical Writer – Mary Sullivan Hutcheson; Technical Associate – Lisa Lancaster; Editorial Writer – Susan Frantz Wiles; Senior Graphic Artist – Lora Puls; Graphic Artists – Cailen Cochran and Leia Morshedi; Photo Stylist - Lori Wenger; Photographer - Ken West.